Contents

The alphabet	2
In the street	6
Songs and rhymes	10
Foz's day	14
At the fair	18
All about books	22
Parent notes	27

Aa Bb Cc Dd Ee
Ff Gg Hh Ii Jj Kk
Ll Mm Nn Oo Pp
Qq Rr Ss Tt Uu
Vv Ww Xx Yy Zz

The alphabet

a → b → c → d

→ e → f → g

h → i → j → k

l m n o → p

The best way to learn the alphabet is by singing it.

▶ Sing the alphabet song as you point to the letters. (Use the tune of Twinkle, Twinkle Little Star.)

▶ Repeat it until your child can sing along with you.

▶ Make a game of stopping part way through the song and asking your child to point to the next letter.

▶ Use the arrows to show your child the left > right direction of print.

Key words
Alphabet, letter.

More activities
See pages 4–5 and 28.

2

w m

Which letter is each animal carrying?

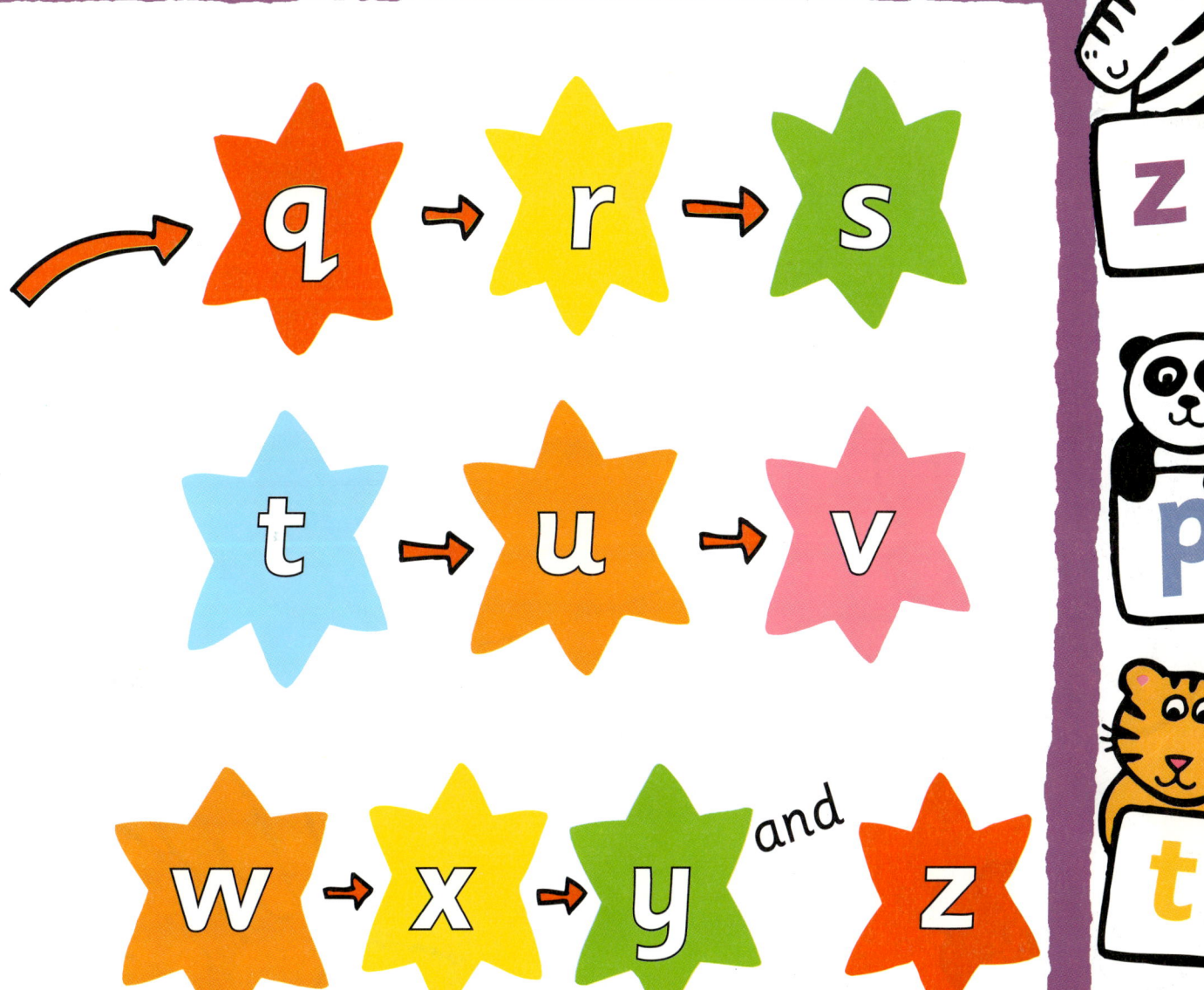

q → r → s

t → u → v

w → x → y and z

Now I know my a b c
Come along and sing with me.

I've done it!

z

p

t

e g s r

3

Join the dots in alphabetical order to make the animals happy.

I've done it!

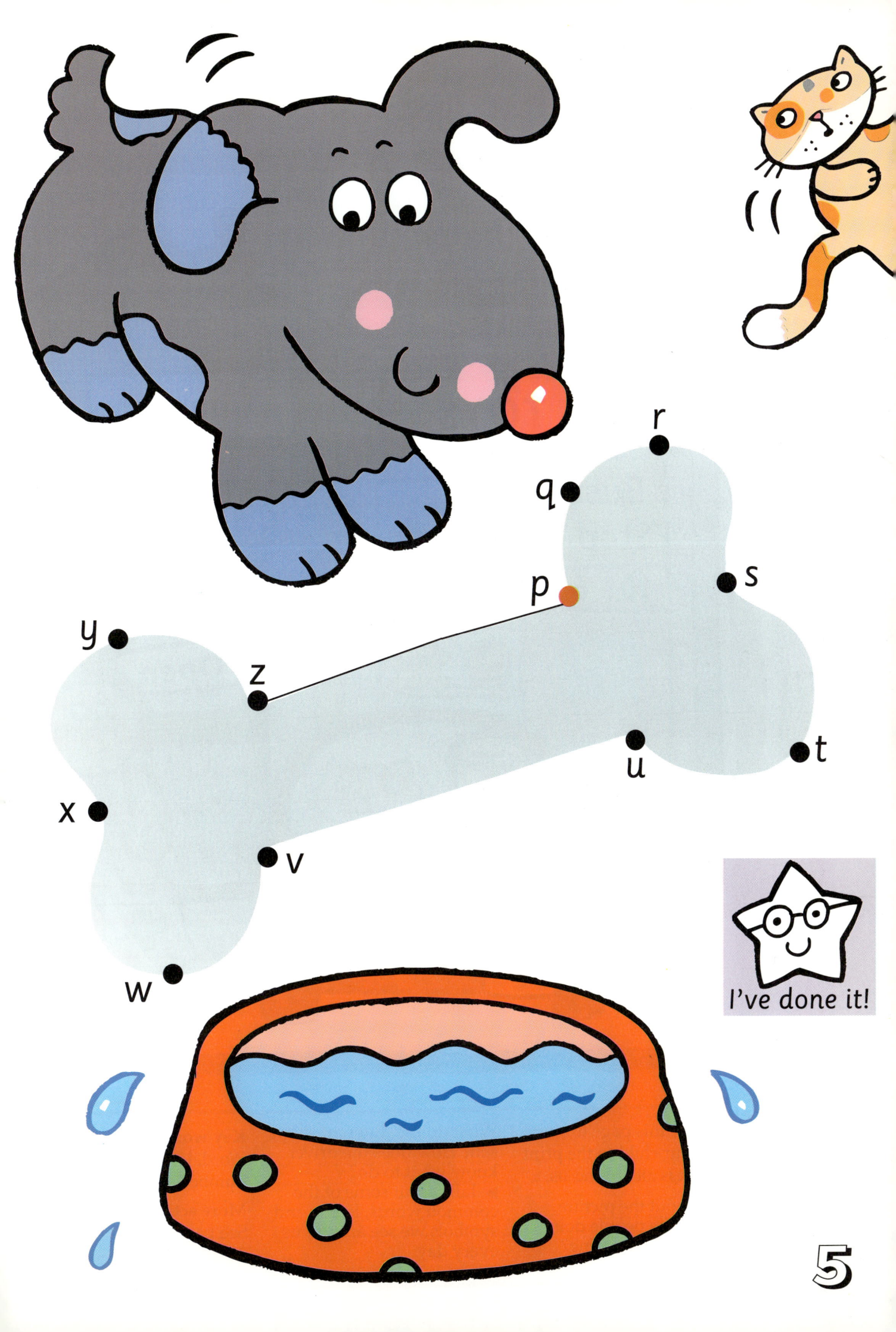

5

In the street

Talk about the picture.

Open

Closed

L

TOYS

Bus Stop
10 6

Chemist

Open

L

Use this page to alert your child to the print that is all around us.

▶ Talk about the picture. What are the people doing? What are they wearing?

What do the different shops sell? How does the driver know what to do?
▶ Talk about some of the common words, letters and symbols we see around us every day.

Key words
Word, letter, number, sign, print.

More activities
See pages 8–9 and 28–29.

Post Office

Burgers

Can you find all these signs in the picture?

Post Office

Burgers

No Dogs

Closed

No Dogs

P

TOYS

HIGH STREET

I've done it!

HIGH STREET

Bus Stop

10 6

7

Draw lines to match the words to the signs. Start at the dots.

Bus Stop

Post Office

No Dogs

HIGH STREET

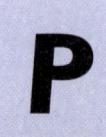

P

Match the letters to the signs.

P   L

Match the words to the doors.

Open

Closed

I've done it!

Songs and rhymes

Old MacDonald had a farm
e i e i o.
And on this farm he had some pigs
e i e i o.

With a grunt grunt here,

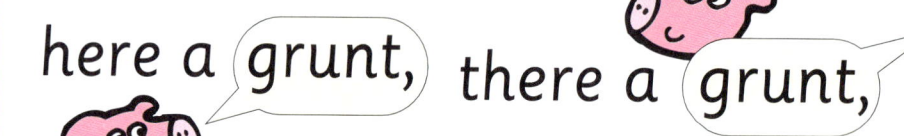

and a grunt grunt there,

here a grunt, there a grunt,

everywhere a grunt grunt.

Old MacDonald had a farm
e i e i o.

Fun activities with sound, rhythm and rhyme prepare children for reading.

With your child:
▶ Sing the song, pointing to the words as you sing.
▶ Point at the speech bubbles on page 11, and make the animal sounds.
▶ Sing the song several times, letting your child choose which animal to sing about by pointing at the relevant animal picture.

Key words
Sound, rhyme.

More activities
See pages 12–13 and 30–31.

What sounds do these animals make?

And on this farm he had some …

hens

cluck cluck
cluck

cows
moo moo
moo

baa baa
baa

woof woof
woof

sheep

dogs

cats
meow meow
meow

squeak squeak
squeak

mice

I've done it!

Do you know these rhymes?

When you can say each rhyme, colour the flag.

Humpty Dumpty

Jack and Jill

The words are on pages 30–31.

Little Bo Peep

Hey Diddle Diddle

Hickory Dickory Dock

Twinkle, Twinkle, Little Star

I've done it!

Mary, Mary, Quite Contrary

Foz's day

Your child has to learn that you read from left to right and from the top to the bottom of the page, and that a story has a beginning, a middle and an end.

▶ 'Read' the story and talk about Foz's day: What does Foz do in the morning? In the afternoon? How is Foz's day the same as and different from yours?

▶ Draw pictures of *your* day.

Key words
Beginning, middle, end, left, right, story.

More activities
See pages 16–17 and 32.

14

Find these things in the story.

I've done it!

Write letters on each row to put the pictures in the right order.

I've done it!

17

At the fair

In

TOILETS

Cafe

Cafe

Telephone

PRIVATE

Out

In

Litter

Some of the first words children learn are the ones they see about them in the everyday world.

▶ Ask questions about the picture: What rides can you see? What are the people doing? What are they wearing?

▶ Point out the signs in the picture and talk about why they are there. How many can your child recognise?

Key words
Word, sign, number, picture, print.

More activities
See pages 20–21 and 28–29.

18

Litter

Ladies

Can you find all these signs in the picture?

Shop

Shop

Out

TOILETS

Ladies   Gentlemen

Exit

I've done it!

PRIVATE

Telephone

19

Draw lines to match the words to the pictures. Start at the dots.

Ladies   Gentlemen   Shop

Litter   PRIVATE

Trace the letters.
Match the words to the pictures.
Start at the dots.

Toilets

Exit

In

Out

I've done it!

21

All about books

a Library	**b**
c Cookery	**d** Children's books

▶ 'Read' the picture story with your child, demonstrating the left > right sequence of the story.

▶ Explain the difference between fiction and non-fiction – story books and information books – and look for examples.

▶ Show how we read fiction and non-fiction differently – e.g. we often don't read a non-fiction book (like a recipe book) in order, but just use the Contents and Index pages to find what we want.

Key words
Fiction, non-fiction.

More activities
See pages 24–25 and 32.

22

Look at the books in the border. Can you find them all in the picture story?

e **Fiction**

f **Non-fiction**

g

h

I've done it!

Match the pages to the books.
Start at the dots.

25

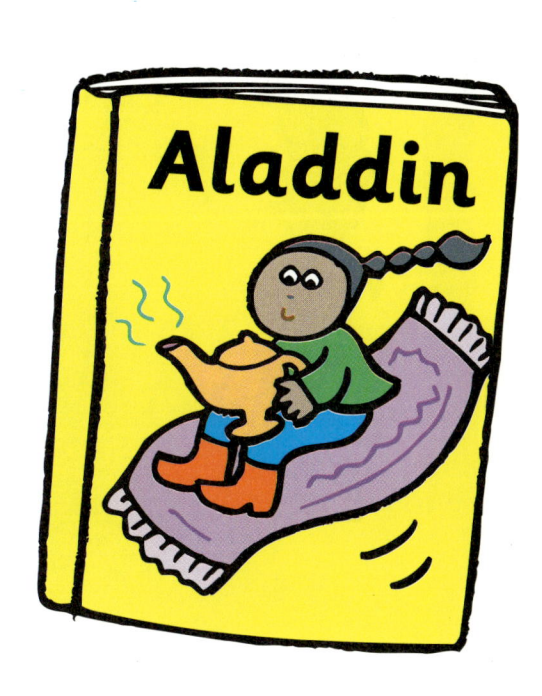

Certificate

Well done!
I can read letters and words.

This is to certify that

_____

is **Ready to Read.**

Fill in your name.

Parent notes

Stages in learning to read

There are many stages in learning to read but the early pre-reading stages are particularly important. Parents can help by laying solid foundations.

Getting ready • Children learn about how language works and develop their vocabulary by talking with parents. They learn about books and stories when their parents read to them.

• They learn the alphabet, and begin to understand what written language is all about, often through reading the print in their everyday environment.

• They become tuned in to the sounds that are important in our language. This is vital if they are later to learn how to 'sound out' words.

Remember also to listen to your child's side of the conversation. To feel at home with language, children need lots of opportunities to practise using it. The best practice comes when they feel their conversation is valued by the adults they love.

Starting to read • When children have had plenty of the sorts of experiences outlined above, they often start reading of their own accord, by joining in with favourite stories and gradually taking over the reading of phrases, sentences and even whole pages for themselves.

• To cope with unfamiliar stories, they must also learn:

the main sounds that individual letters stand for;
sounds made by common combinations of letters (e.g. sh, ch, th);
that patterns of sound can be reflected in patterns of letters (e.g. cat, sat, mat);
that common words must be recognised as wholes (not sounded out);
that reading involves combining many skills, in the way that suits their brain the best!

Developing language • The skills of reading and writing are built upon children's spoken English – so progress depends on plenty of opportunities to practise both speaking and listening. Your child needs your attention and interest – conversation widens his or her knowledge of the world and teaches the words with which to talk about it.

• As well as talking about your day-to-day life, you can extend your child's horizons by sharing picture books, video and multimedia. The important thing is to talk about what you read and view – and listen to what your child has to say.

The alphabet

pages 2–5

To start with, your child needs help with getting to know the letter names and recognising the letter shapes that go with them. This is quite a task – it involves learning 26 meaningless sounds and peculiar squiggles! And it's 52 squiggles if you count the capital letters – which is why most teachers recommend sticking with the small letters to begin with.

Ideas
- Put up an alphabet frieze in your child's room.
- Make an alphabet frieze of your own, with pictures for each letter, drawn by members of the family.
- Play 'Spot the letter' when you're out and about – choosing a particular letter and looking for it in shop signs and so on.
- Look at a variety of alphabet books from the local library.

There are lots of ways of appealing to children's interests. Your child could make an alphabet frieze from chocolate and biscuit wrappers – which he or she could have had great fun compiling!

Remember
- To start with, teach your child the letters and their names.
- Stick with the lower-case letters wherever possible.

Print all around

pages 6–9, 18–21

It can take quite a while for children to recognise that the squiggles they see on paper represent language – the same thing they hear people speaking. A good way to help them see that printed words carry a message is to point out the words in their everyday environment.

Shop and street signs are simple, highly meaningful examples of print – and they often carry messages which are very important to a child. Many children recognise words like 'Stop', 'Playground' and 'Park' at quite an early age.

The more we talk to children about the print they see around them, the more they're likely to notice it and recognise that it has a message to convey.

Ideas
- Play 'Spot the sign' when you're out (e.g. 'How many FOR SALE signs are there in this road?' 'How many OPEN signs can you find on shop doors?').
- Point out the same word in different contexts (e.g. 'stop' on the lollipop sign and on the bus stop; 'sale' in FOR SALE signs and SALE in shop windows).
- Talk about why some letters stand for words (e.g. P is for 'parking', because the word 'parking' starts with a P sound).

- Another sort of everyday print many children notice quite early is the print on food wrappers! Draw attention to familiar letters (e.g. the M for M&S is the same letter as the M in M&Ms).

What about capitals?

Many of the words on street signs are in capital letters. In the early stages, this doesn't matter – children do not associate the signs they see with the individual alphabet letters but take them in as wholes, and respond to the meaning.

Once you are looking at and talking about letters, first concentrate on words in which the capital version of the first letter looks similar to the small form (e.g. M, S and P). Later, explain that there are two ways of writing letters.

Words to spot

Don't try to do too many at once. One new sign per outing is enough – and let your child point out the ones he or she knows already.

In the street	In the shops	At the park	Other words
No Parking	Pull	Park	Happy Birthday
Car park	Push	Playground	Love
STOP	Pay here	Way out	Merry Christmas
Bus stop	No Smoking	Keep out	Party
FOR SALE	SALE	No entry	Today
School	EXIT	Ladies	Private
WAIT	FIRE EXIT	Gentlemen	Play
Open	Emergency	Toilets	Record
Closed	Toilets	Ice Cream	Stop
Fish and chips	Baby changing room	Snacks	Good Food
Post Office	Sweets	No dogs	

Individual letters

M for M&S	I for Information	B&B for Bed and Breakfast
L for Learner	P for Parking	H for Hydrant

Sounds, rhythm and rhyme

pages 2–3, 10–13

Before children can learn to read, their ears must be tuned in to the sounds which are important in language. They must also become aware of the rhythms of speech and the sorts of patterns we can make in speaking, through repeating a sound, a word or a phrase.

For generations, parents have prepared their children to read by sharing songs, nursery rhymes and jingles. These have all the ingredients to train infant ears – strong rhythms, lots of repetition, plenty of rhyme (think of Humpty Dumpty and Mary Mary, Quite Contrary) and alliteration (repetition of the same letter – **J**ack and **J**ill, **S**ing a **S**ong of **S**ixpence).

Singing favourite rhymes over and over again helps children to memorise them – this trains their memory for sound, which is vitally important to reading. Reciting from memory as you point to the words is for many children the first step on the way to cracking the code.

Unfortunately, in these days of video and daytime TV, the old rhymes can be neglected. (Rhymes on screen are nowhere near as effective – unless an adult is sharing them with the child.) Sharing is the key ingredient. With you to encourage and repeat the rhyme as often as he or she wants, your child can gradually join in, and pick up the words and tune. There is plenty of fun to be had with song, rhyme and rhythm.

Ideas
- Sing or recite a familiar rhyme, missing out words for your child to supply.
- Play 'Guess the rhyme', using pictures (see pages 12–13) or by acting out the story.
- Look in the library for action rhymes, which help develop coordination as well as memory.

Old favourites It's worth investing in a good nursery rhyme book, which you and your child can browse through, gradually building up a repertoire. The rhymes on pages 10–13 are some old favourites. Here are the full texts:

Humpty Dumpty sat on a wall,
Humpty Dumpty had a great fall.
All the king's horses
And all the king's men
Couldn't put Humpty together again.

Twinkle, twinkle, little star,
How I wonder what you are.
Up above the world so high
Like a diamond in the sky.
Twinkle, twinkle, little star,
How I wonder what you are.

Hey diddle diddle,
The cat and the fiddle,
The cow jumped over the moon.
The little dog laughed
To see such fun,
And the dish ran away with the spoon.

Hickory dickory dock,
The mouse ran up the clock.
The clock struck one,
The mouse ran down,
Hickory dickory dock.

Jack and Jill went up the hill
To fetch a pail of water.
Jack fell down and broke his crown
And Jill came tumbling after.

Mary, Mary, quite contrary,
How does your garden grow?
With silver bells
And cockle shells
And pretty maids all in a row.

Little Bo Peep has lost her sheep
And doesn't know where to find them.
Leave them alone, and they'll come home,
Wagging their tails behind them.

Don't forget the following:

Sing a song of sixpence	Ding dong bell
Mary had a little lamb	Pussy cat, pussy cat
Rock-a-bye baby	This little piggy
Little Tommy Tucker	Tom, Tom, the piper's son
Incy Wincy Spider	The Grand Old Duke of York
Ride a cockhorse	There was an old woman who swallowed a fly
Georgie Porgie	The old woman who lived in a shoe
The house that Jack built	Oranges and Lemons
Ring a ring o' roses	Little Miss Muffet
Pat-a-cake, pat-a-cake	The Queen of Hearts
Wee Willie Winkie	

How books work

pages 14–17, 22–25

Learning to read isn't just about letters and words. Children must learn lots of other things about books and print – like the simple fact that, in English, writing starts at the top of the page and the words go across from left to right until you reach the bottom.

Children need help in finding out the most elementary things – which way up to hold a book, how it opens and where to find the beginning and the end. They also have to learn that there are many sorts of books – story books, poem books, cookery books, encyclopedias – and many ways of reading them. The way you read an Agatha Christie, for instance, is very different from the way you read the Yellow Pages.

The best way to teach all this is by example – by reading to your child every day, and sometimes taking the trouble to talk about what you do. This helps him or her to learn important words about reading, like 'page', 'line', 'word' and 'letter'. (See 'The language of print' below.)

Ideas
- Join the local library and let your child help you choose books as soon as he or she is able. (There are often story-telling sessions and other events in children's libraries, which your child might enjoy.)

- Help your child to make his or her own books. Use folded paper and let your child draw the pictures while you write the words he or she suggests. Make an attractive front cover with your child's name on it, and read the book together.

- Include books among birthday and Christmas presents for your child, and help him or her build up a small personal library – returning to favourite books again and again helps build a firm foundation for reading.

- Look at the covers of books when you're choosing them, and ask what your child thinks they'll be about, and why.

- Point out to your child how you use books in daily life – like consulting recipes or computer manuals, using the telephone directory, or browsing through a magazine. All this shows children what reading is for, and why it's so important to everybody.

Above all, try to ensure that your child's experience of books, reading and print is always positive and enjoyable. Happy children make the best progress, and a child who thinks reading is fun is already halfway to becoming a reader.

The language of print Some of the key words children need to know about reading and writing are:

- letter • word • sound • line • page • space • top • bottom
- beginning • middle • end • title • sign • number • picture
- symbol • print • full stop • capital letter • story • rhyme • poem
- song • fiction • non-fiction • contents